NATURAL DISASTERS
MEETING THE CHA[LLENGE]

MW01044878

FLOOD
READINESS

Natalie Hyde
Crabtree Publishing Company
www.crabtreebooks.com

CRABTREE
PUBLISHING COMPANY
WWW.CRABTREEBOOKS.COM

Author: Natalie Hyde

Series research and development:
Janine Deschenes, Reagan Miller

Editorial director: Kathy Middleton

Editors: Ellen Rodger, Melissa Boyce

Proofreader: Wendy Scavuzzo

Design and photo research:
Margaret Amy Salter
Katherine Berti

Prepress technician:
Tammy McGarr

Print and production coordinator:
Katherine Berti

Images:

Associated Press: Martin Mejia: p. 19 (top)
Commonwealth of Australia (Geoscience Australia) 2019: p. 27 (inset)
FEMA: Jocelyn Augustino: front cover (bottom)
iStockphoto: benedek: p. 23 (top right)
NASA GFMS: p. 24
NOAA National Severe Storm Laboratory: p. 32
Shutterstock
 AJP: p. 34
 Angel L: p. 39
 APN Photography: p. 12
 Aranya 22: p. 33
 Chatchai Somwat: p. 11, 35
 Ian Tessier: p. 31 (bottom)
Justina Elgaafary: p. 15
MISHELLA: p. 40 (top)
michelmond: p. 4
northallertonman: p. 25 (top)
PhilMacDPhoto: p. 25 (bottom)
Robert Hiette: p. 26 (both)
Victor Wong: p. 21
Wutthichai: p. 1
zixia: p. 42
Wikimedia Commons
 Ben Record: p. 20
 Cintos (Michael Davias): p. 29
 Ministerio Bienes Nacionales: p. 10
 RAF-YYC from Calgary, Canada: p. 23 (bottom)
 Ryan L. C. Quan: p. 22
All other images by Shutterstock

Library and Archives Canada Cataloguing in Publication

Title: Flood readiness / Natalie Hyde.
Names: Hyde, Natalie, 1963- author.
Description: Series statement: Natural disasters: meeting the challenge | Includes bibliographical references and index.
Identifiers: Canadiana (print) 20190134313 | Canadiana (ebook) 20190134321 | ISBN 9780778765059 (hardcover) | ISBN 9780778765271 (softcover) | ISBN 9781427123794 (HTML)
Subjects: LCSH: Floods—Juvenile literature. | LCSH: Emergency management—Juvenile literature.
Classification: LCC GB1399 .H93 2019 | DDC j551.48/9—dc23

Library of Congress Cataloging-in-Publication Data

Names: Hyde, Natalie, 1963- author.
Title: Flood readiness / Natalie Hyde.
Description: New York, New York : Crabtree Publishing Company, [2020] | Series: Natural disasters: meeting the challenge | Includes bibliographical references and index.
Identifiers: LCCN 2019026946 (print) | LCCN 2019026947 (ebook) | ISBN 9780778765059 (hardcover) | ISBN 9780778765271 (paperback) | ISBN 9781427123794 (ebook)
Subjects: LCSH: Flood control--Juvenile literature. | Floods--Juvenile literature.
Classification: LCC TC530 .H93 2020 (print) | LCC TC530 (ebook) | DDC 363.34/93--dc23
LC record available at https://lccn.loc.gov/2019026946
LC ebook record available at https://lccn.loc.gov/2019026947

Crabtree Publishing Company

www.crabtreebooks.com   1-800-387-7650

Printed in the U.S.A./102019/CG20190809

Copyright © **2020 CRABTREE PUBLISHING COMPANY.** All rights reserved. No part of this publication may be reproduced, stored in a retrieval system or be transmitted in any form or by any means, electronic, mechanical, photocopying, recording, or otherwise, without the prior written permission of Crabtree Publishing Company. In Canada: We acknowledge the financial support of the Government of Canada through the Canada Book Fund for our publishing activities.

Published in Canada
Crabtree Publishing
616 Welland Ave.
St. Catharines, Ontario
L2M 5V6

Published in the United States
Crabtree Publishing
PMB 59051
350 Fifth Avenue, 59th Floor
New York, New York 10118

Published in the United Kingdom
Crabtree Publishing
Maritime House
Basin Road North, Hove
BN41 1WR

Published in Australia
Crabtree Publishing
Unit 3–5 Currumbin Court
Capalaba
QLD 4157

Contents

Are Floods Unavoidable?

Nature can be unpredictable. Sometimes events happen that cause **severe** damage to buildings and **infrastructure**, as well as injuries and loss of life. These are called disasters. Floods can become disasters when they disrupt normal ways of life.

How They Happen

Water is everywhere on our planet. Flooding happens when water covers land that is usually dry. It is one of the most common and most destructive types of natural disasters. This is because many factors can cause flooding. Heavy rainstorms can cause rivers and canals to overflow. Dams that control the flow of water or that are used to generate power can burst. That sends a sudden violent surge of water downstream.

Climate Change

As our climate changes, glaciers high in the mountains are melting at a faster rate, often sending water down into valleys faster than the waterways can handle. Violent storms such as hurricanes or winds, and rainy seasons such as monsoons, dump large amounts of rain, flooding land and turning streets into rivers.

*Residents walk across a flooded street in Houston, Texas. Heavy rains from Hurricane Harvey in 2017 caused many **urban** areas to flood. The water had nowhere to drain.*

Many cities around the world are built on floodplains. For these communities, flooding can be a natural part of the environment, such as this flood that occurred in Brisbane in Queensland, Australia in 2011.

Human Settlement and Water

Flooding affects millions of people each year because so many people live close to water.

Many towns and cities were historically built near water sources such as rivers, lakes, and ocean shorelines. Before there were cars, trains, and planes, waterways were transportation routes. People traveled from place to place using waterways as highways.

Rivers, lakes, and streams provided fresh drinking water, as well as irrigation for crops. Water forms a natural barrier— keeping invaders out. Many port cities were built on sheltered bays.

Floodplains

Today, many towns and cities are still near water. Some are on or near existing or ancient floodplains. These are areas near rivers that experience flooding. As populations grew, humans changed the landscape to better suit roads, parks, and homes. In doing so, we changed the route water can flow. **Dikes** and **levees** allow people and businesses to build in dangerous flood zones. When these protective structures fail, it is a bigger disaster because more people are in the danger zone.

Everyone Is at Risk

Flooding is a worldwide problem. There is almost no place on Earth where it is not a threat. Storms and heavy rainfall can affect all areas. Even deserts can experience floods. The dry and often rocky ground does not soak up rainfall very well, so it begins flowing on the surface. With no plants to slow it down, the water races across the desert, sweeping away soil and rocks and causing erosion.

People living in mountains are at risk when snow and ice begin to melt. If the temperature rises too quickly, the **meltwater** will race down and flood valleys where towns have developed. On the coast, severe storms can send a wall of water onto the shore, flooding farmland and cities.

Flooding Vulnerability

Flooding kills people and causes billions of dollars in damage to homes and property around the world each year. Flooding disasters also disrupt lives. People may have to be evacuated to safer areas, leaving their homes, jobs, and support networks. Flooding damages or destroys infrastructure such as roads, bridges, railway tracks, ports, and airport runways. It overwhelms sewage treatment systems, resulting in contaminated drinking water. In some places, this can result in the spread of diseases such as typhoid or hepatitis.

$1.7 TRILLION

The total cost of 250 weather and climate events, including flooding, since 1980

ROAD CLOSED

When roads are destroyed or under water, it is hard for food, clothing, water, and medicine to reach people affected by the flood.

CASE STUDY
WMO and Flood Management

The World Meteorological Organization (WMO) is a special branch of the **United Nations**. It helps countries work together to **predict**, warn, and prepare for severe weather. The Volta River Basin is one of the largest river systems in Africa. It is spread across six West African countries. More than 14 million people live in the river basin and are at risk each year from flooding. In 2018 alone, 34 people were killed and 52,000 lost their homes and property. The Volta Basin Project, headed by the WMO, will help the area with the first large-scale strategies for **forecasting** floods and **droughts**. Gauges along the river system will monitor water levels to warn of high water. Reports of rising water will give residents time to protect their homes, land, livestock, and families before the flood begins. After flooding, the plans will help people, supplies, and equipment quickly get to the areas needing help.

River water level gauges

The African country of

GHANA

lies in the Volta River Basin. Between

1991 and 2011

Ghana experienced

7 MAJOR FLOODS

CHAPTER 1

The Science Behind Flooding

There are many factors that cause flooding. An imbalance in the water cycle can cause problems. Too much rain will cause a delay in water soaking into the ground. Too little rain and the ground becomes dry and hard. When it rains again, this ground will not **absorb** water very well. Lots of rain in an area that does not normally get rain means the water systems and surrounding land cannot absorb the water quickly. These factors, combined with human-made problems, result in water flowing where it is normally dry. Often several different factors, both natural and human-made, all come together to cause floods.

The Water Cycle

Most of the surface of planet Earth is covered in water. That water is never still—it is always moving in a cycle.

The water cycle begins with evaporation. This is when water is heated by the Sun and it turns to steam or vapor. As the vapor rises in the air, it cools and forms clouds. Cooled vapor turns back into liquid water. This is called condensation. As the drops collect together in clouds, they become too heavy to stay in the air. The drops fall as rain. Then the cycle starts all over again.

The Water Cycle

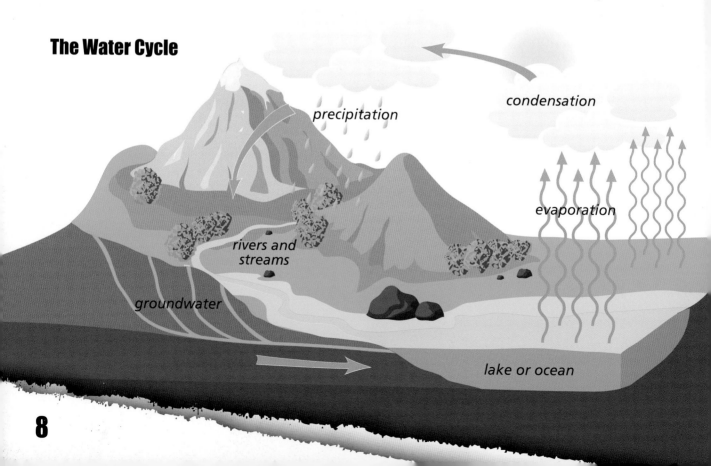

condensation

precipitation

evaporation

rivers and streams

groundwater

lake or ocean

River Flooding

There are different types of floods. River flooding is the most common type. During this type of flood, the water level in a river rises slowly until it climbs over its banks and floods the surrounding area.

Coastal Flooding

Coastal flooding occurs during severe storms. Seawater is pushed onto land by heavy winds or high tides. In cities, sewers and drains can flood when there is a blockage so the water cannot flow. They can also flood if there is too much water at one time for the system to handle, causing it to back up.

Flash Floods

Flash floods are more dangerous. The water rises suddenly and with very little warning, quickly sweeping over an area. Flash floods do not give people time to prepare. Flooding happens more quickly in areas where water cannot soak into the ground fast enough. Water builds up very quickly in low areas on roads and highways, and in city centers with large areas of concrete and pavement.

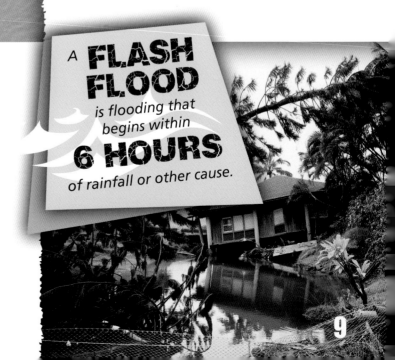

A **FLASH FLOOD** is flooding that begins within **6 HOURS** of rainfall or other cause.

What Causes Flooding?

Floods can happen because of one factor or when many factors combine at the same time. Some factors are natural. Landforms, weather, and climate are all natural factors that play a part in flooding.

One of the most common factors for flooding is heavy rainfall. Heavy rainfall creates the conditions for river flooding and flash flooding. Rain is a natural part of the water cycle. Rain falls in all areas of the world. Even deserts have a small amount of rain each year. Different areas are used to getting different amounts of rain. Rain forests get a lot of rain. Their dense tree growth with many roots soak up the rain. There are also rivers to move the extra water out of the area.

Atacama Flooding

Deserts do not get a lot of rain. There, the sandy soil can easily handle a small amount of water, but is overrun when heavy rains hit. The Atacama Desert in Chile, South America, had not had a significant rainfall in 500 years. In June 2017, heavy rains created flooding across the desert. Temporary lakes formed in low areas. Instead of bringing life to the desert, the sudden water killed most of the **microscopic life** that was used to extremely dry conditions.

Almost

3,000 PEOPLE

were forced to leave their homes after flooding in the Atacama Desert region in 2017.

Meltwater runoff becomes even worse when a heavy spring rain falls on the snow cover. The combination creates some of the worst floods.

Sky-High Snow

Some floods happen when winter snows melt. Heavy snows and a fast melt in spring mean the ground is saturated, or soaked. Too much snowmelt can lead to floods. Snowfall is heavier in mountainous regions. In some mountain ranges, such as the Cascades in Washington, snow cover can be up to 95 feet (29 m) high! If temperatures rise quickly in spring, too much meltwater flows and floods nearby rivers and streams.

Red Cross supplies for flood victims in Bangkok, Thailand, 2011

SCIENCE BIO
Global Flood Awareness System

The Global Flood Awareness (GFA) system is used by the **Red Cross/Red Crescent** Climate Center. When a flood is predicted, this system allows organizations to begin programs that help flood victims before the flood even happens. Once the flood hits, roads and runways are often not usable. In an area likely to flood, the Red Cross can give out tablets to purify water in anticipation of sewage backups.

Spring Floods

Where rain falls is as much a factor as how much rain falls. If the water cannot drain away, flooding will happen. Some soils, such as clay, do not absorb water well. Water stays on the ground longer and collects in low-lying areas, raising water levels. Soil that is frozen can also not absorb water. In the spring, air temperatures may rise high enough for rain to fall instead of snow, but the ground can still be frozen. Any rainfall will stay on the surface. This is one reason why many severe floods happen in the spring.

MARCH 2019

Heavy winter rains in the midwestern U.S. raised water levels on the Missouri River to more than 30 feet (9 m).

Ice jams reduce the flow of a river, which can then lead to upstream flooding.

Ice Jams

Flooding can be the result of another springtime event—ice jams on rivers. As the ice on frozen rivers melts, it breaks into large pieces that begin to move downstream. Sometimes these blocks of ice get stuck and dam up the river. This causes all the water above the ice jam to back up and spill over the riverbank, flooding fields, homes, and roads.

Sudden Rushes

When the ice jam breaks, a huge amount of water that had been held back suddenly rushes forward. This sudden gush of water and ice chunks can cause damage downstream. Sometimes, communities use explosives to break up the ice jams before they can cause too many problems.

Ice isn't the only kind of dam to cause a risk of flooding when it breaks. Large beaver dams or even human-made dams that produce electricity, such as the Hoover Dam on the Colorado River, can fail, sending a flash flood downstream.

Human Factors

Human actions are also factors in flooding. Every time people alter landforms and landscapes, build new highways, or expand cities, we increase our risk of flooding. Large cities are a collection of buildings and roads that cover huge areas of soil with concrete, bricks, and pavement. Water has very few places where it can seep into the ground. Most rain is collected in gutters and eaves troughs, which empty into sewers. The water is directed through pipes away from the city center into nearby streams, rivers, or canals. Sewer pipes can only handle a limited amount of water. Excess water floods roads and basements.

Natural Flooding

Some rivers and streams naturally flood every year. For thousands of years, the Nile River in Egypt flooded every spring. Floodwaters carried rich **sediment** onto the flat areas on both sides of the river. These are called floodplains. Egyptians used these plains to grow crops because the flooding made the soil fertile. But the ancient Egyptians did not build their homes or temples on the floodplains. Today, as cities and towns throughout the world grow, roads and buildings are sometimes built on or very near floodplains. These areas are at risk of floods. Without natural floodplains, high river water has to find somewhere else to go.

Rainwater is directed away from city centers through pipes which empty into streams, rivers, or canals.

The village of Armant, Egypt, sits on the shore of the Nile River.

Climate Change

Humans have affected the natural cycle of flooding in other ways. Through our use of **fossil fuels**, rising pollution, and **deforestation**, our climate is changing. This means weather patterns and the water cycle are also changing. Heavy rains are falling in areas that did not normally get a lot of rain. Storms are becoming more severe. Earth's temperature is rising, leading to the polar ice caps melting. This is raising sea levels. With higher seas and higher tides, coastal areas are experiencing more flooding more often.

Egyptians built several dams to manage the flood-and-drought cycle of the Nile. The Aswan High Dam was the most recent. Unfortunately, the silt and sediment that made the soil so rich for farming is now deposited behind the dam.

SCIENCE BIO
Urban Flood Management

Chris Zevenbergen is a professor at the IHE Delft Institute for Water Education in Delft, The Netherlands. He has been an advisor and manager for many projects dealing with flood management. He researches how to handle the effects of flooding in cities.

He also works with construction companies to flood-proof buildings. Zevenbergen sits on many boards to advise governments and scientific groups. He has also published five books to share what he has learned about **urban** flood management.

Flood management projects can be used to prepare cities such as Alexandria, Egypt, when it experiences floods like this one in 2016.

CHAPTER 2

Studying Disasters and Their Effects

Floods have always been a problem for humans. Before people had a way to predict floods or try to manage floodwater, they affected millions of people. These floods drove people to try to create systems and machinery that could help warn others of coming dangers.

The floods of the Yangtze River in China covered an area the size of England and half of Scotland combined.

Scotland

England

Great Flood of China

In 1931, a series of events—drought, heavy snow and rains, then severe **cyclones**—led to one of the deadliest floods in history in the Republic of China. The excess water had the Yangtze River rising to its highest level since people began to keep records in the area.

Poor Flood Management

Researchers say the disaster was mostly caused by human activity. Over time, farmers had cleared forests, which help slow and absorb rainfall. People had built homes and farms on floodplains and in **wetlands**. They built dikes to control small floods, but had neglected them over time. When the heavy melted snow and severe storms combined, the dikes failed and the people living in the flood zone were trapped.

52 MILLION
people were affected by the flood.

2 MILLION
people died from drowning, starvation, and disease brought by the flood.

Unprepared for Disaster

China was not equipped to handle the disaster. The country had difficulty getting food, clean drinking water, and medicine into communities. As a result of the flood, the Chinese government created the National Flood Relief Commission. This organization used experts from all over the world to help collect and distribute supplies. The dikes were also rebuilt. Unfortunately, forests were still cleared and building in flood zones was still permitted. In 1935, the dikes failed again during a period of heavy rainfall and the area flooded again. Flood management was still simple for many years after.

After the Flood

Until recently, China's flood management was simple. During the spring, flood control officers would walk the dikes to watch for rising water levels. Now, smartphones collect data from hundreds of stations to monitor water levels. Drones are also used to report on floods and remote-controlled rescue robots shaped like lifeboats can rescue stranded people and deliver supplies.

The Year of Floods

Sometimes it is not just one area that experiences flooding. In 1998, flooding was a disaster that affected almost all parts of our planet. North America, South America, Asia, and Europe all faced record-setting rainfall and river levels.

Rain and Damage

In October 1998, Texas and Kansas experienced severe flooding after heavy rains. In Texas, 25 people died and hundreds of millions of dollars in damage was reported. The Halloween Flood in Kansas forced thousands of people to **evacuate**. Heavy rains in Peru and Ecuador in South America led to coastal flooding that washed away bridges, crops, homes, and roads. In Africa, flooding in Kenya washed out runways and roads. Asia also had severe flooding. China's floods in 1998 left almost 4,000 people dead and 15 million people homeless. Bangladesh, England, Australia, Brazil, India, and Japan also experienced damaging floods that year.

Weather Whys

Scientists tried to explain why severe weather and heavy rainfall affected so many parts of the world in one year. They point to the fact that a weather event called El Niño happened in 1997–1998. El Niño is an area of warmer-than-normal water in the Pacific Ocean that causes changes in weather patterns. Warmer air picks up more water vapor, which creates heavier rain.

The government in China also admitted that deforestation contributed to the problem in their country. Trees take in carbon dioxide and give off oxygen. Higher levels of carbon dioxide cause global temperatures to rise, leading to climate change such as more violent storms. Scientists warn that with increasing global warming, intense storms and heavier rainfall will become even more common. Years of flooding, such as 1998, have helped more people and more countries face the reality of climate change and motivate them to do something about it.

18.7 MILLION ACRES (7.6 MILLION HECTARES)

of forests are lost each year due to deforestation.

Areas of Peru, in South America, were affected by flooding caused by heavy rains that were attributed to the weather event El Niño in 1998.

Flood Control

Many cities and regions that are at a high risk of flooding build structures for protection. The Netherlands has a network of dikes to keep seawater out of homes and streets. Canals, like those in England, can help control the amount of water flowing through areas. Reservoirs, or artificial lakes, are designed to hold back water to keep levels stable. But the only way to know if these structures are strong enough or built properly is to test them with a real flood.

When the Levees Failed

The city of New Orleans, Louisiana, was built in the marshy floodplain of the Mississippi River **delta**. To protect the city from floods, levees and floodwalls were built. As the swamplands were drained so the city could grow, the area began to sink. Reports suggested more than half of the city was now below sea level. If the levees failed, the flooding would be severe.

People living in the areas were led to believe they were safe, and that the levees and floodwalls would hold. But when Hurricane Katrina hit the area in 2005, the rain and wind were too much. The levees failed and 80 percent of the city flooded.

Almost 2,000 people died during Hurricane Katrina and in the floods that happened afterward. Investigations later said the levees failed in more than 50 places.

The **$14.5 BILLION WEST CLOSURE COMPLEX** was built in a ring around New Orleans to reduce the risk of flooding from hurricanes and **storm surges**.

Investigating the Failure

Some people believed a huge flood was bound to happen because three sides of the city were bordered by water and most of the city was below sea level. But a report by a group of civil engineers concluded that if the levees, floodwalls, and pumping stations hadn't failed, two-thirds of the deaths wouldn't have happened.

Rebuilding for Flooding

Since the flooding, the levees have been rebuilt. But reports by the National Academy of Engineering state that in another major storm, the rebuilt floodwalls and levees will likely fail again. With rising sea levels and more severe storms, the price of building adequate protection is so high that Louisiana has chosen to make adjustments to the levees already there.

21

No Way Out

The "flood of all floods" in Alberta, Canada, began with heavy snowfall in October 2012. By the following spring, the snowpack was more than 3 feet (1 m) deep in places. This was followed by heavy rains throughout spring 2013. The rains caused massive floods and landslides that closed Canada's biggest highway, the Trans-Canada Highway. People had to be rescued using helicopters, boats, and farm equipment such as manure spreaders. The Bow River that flows through the city of Calgary overtopped its banks, and 3,000 buildings were flooded. **Debris** clogged and damaged roads, bridges, and railway tracks.

5 PEOPLE lost their lives as a result of the Alberta flood of 2013 and damages cost **$6 BILLION.**

CASE STUDY
Global Water Futures

A $78-million study by the University of Saskatchewan will help it lead the largest water project in the world. Working with three other universities in Canada, the Global Water Futures project will improve ways to predict water-related threats. It will research ways to limit the damage from droughts and floods. The study will also examine water-quality hazards on Indigenous lands where water quality is hazardous. New technology will be used, including **acoustic** snow sensors and drone sensors to measure snow depth and density.

University of Saskatchewan

In Calgary's Saddledome arena, where the Calgary Flames hockey team plays, water reached the tenth row of seats.

Flood Barriers

During the flood, Calgary lowered the level in the Glenmore Reservoir to make room for more water. Flood barriers were also built in certain areas. While these actions helped a little, the river still spilled over into the nearby Bow and Elbow rivers. A new flood plan has been created to help prevent future floods. That plan includes two new reservoirs upriver from the city. Calgary will also build new flood barriers near the core of the city and improve the drainage system. Almost half the residents of Alberta also now have flood insurance, which will help them after future floods.

23

CHAPTER 3

Meeting the Challenge

Scientists tell us that with climate change, flooding will become a bigger issue in the future. We are all going to have to learn how to live with an increased risk to our homes, property, and lives. To reduce risk, researchers are developing new systems that track different kinds of information that help predict the possibility of flooding.

Flood Prediction

Flood prediction isn't like using a crystal ball. Scientists use information from past floods, the "behavior" of water bodies, and other factors to help determine the likely size and extent of some floods. Behavior means the patterns rivers, lakes, and ocean waters follow during times of excess water. Some of the other factors examined are:

- The amount of rainfall as it is falling
- How quickly water levels are rising
- The type of storm and how much rain it usually brings
- The area the storm covers, and how long it might last
- The type of soil, ground temperature, size of forests, risk of erosion in the area
- Changes to the area due to deforestation, farming, or erosion

The Global Flood Monitoring System sponsored by NASA maps flood conditions in real time. It uses rainfall, plant cover, soil type, and landforms to figure out how much water is soaking in and how much is flowing. The information is combined and shown on a map.

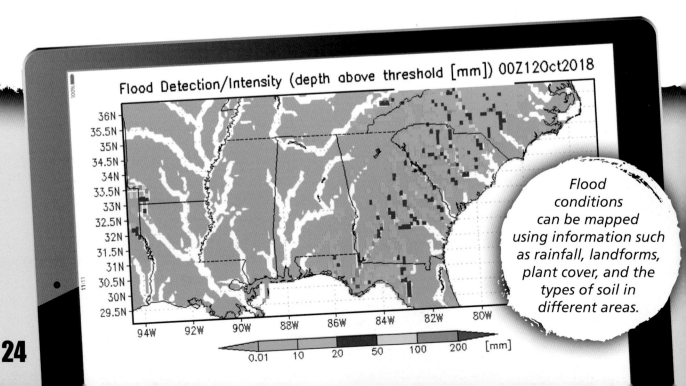

Flood conditions can be mapped using information such as rainfall, landforms, plant cover, and the types of soil in different areas.

The city of York, England, was flooded in 2018 after heavy rains caused rivers in the area to overflow.

The British Army and mountain rescue teams were sent to York to evacuate residents from the city.

New Models for Prediction

Engineers at the Ruhr University Bochum in Germany have also developed a new flood prediction system. In this model, they can keep watch on three different types of flood factors: short heavy rainfall, rainfall over several days, and snowmelt. They combine these factors with knowledge of the landscape and soils in different flood areas. The program can calculate flood risk if there is heavy rain in an area with one river and clay soil, or if it is a large river system with many **tributaries**. Right now, they only have data for certain parts of the country but will be expanding the program for all of Germany in the near future.

Flood Network

The United Kingdom has created a Flood Network system. Residents, businesses, or organizations can install wireless sensors near waterways, rivers, or ditches. The sensor sends data to a central system over the Internet. With this information, it creates an online map that updates water levels every 15 minutes. It can send alerts to users if the water is rising or reaches a certain level.

Watch and Learn

Once a river has begun to rise and spill over its banks, it is important for the flood to be tracked and monitored. Some floods only affect small or rural areas. In that case, fewer people are in danger and the flood won't have a big impact on roads, farms, or buildings. Other floods happen in or near cities, major highways, and airports. Some floods can also hit tourist areas or beaches. Managing these disasters takes a lot of organization to evacuate people or arrange emergency rescues.

Rising floodwaters in Townsville, Queensland, Australia threaten a bridge and homes after a monsoon trough, or winds that push rains, pounded the area with heavy rain.

The Australian Army assists in the cleanup after the flooding.

Sensor Alerts

In the Philippines, a system is being tested that allows people to get timely flood information without the Internet. It is seen as useful for saving the lives of people in remote or poorer areas who do not have home computers. This new system uses sensors placed along waterways. These sensors monitor water levels. If a flood is detected, the system sends a text message to local officials and agencies. Information can be shared to alert residents when floodwaters are getting close, or when areas with only one way in or out might be cut off.

Artificial Intelligence

Some newer flood alert systems are using **artificial intelligence** to look for patterns in past floods to predict what will happen in the future. Researchers at Stanford University in California are working on this early warning system that can predict how bad flooding will be up to five days in advance of a storm. This gives people time to prepare their homes, move their cars, and pack up their pets.

Using SAR to Track Floods

In Australia, a flood in the northeastern state of Queensland early in 2019 was so large that the usual way of using airplanes to map the area wasn't useful. The flood covered more than 434 miles (700 km) of coastline. It would have taken days to map the whole flood zone. Instead, European satellites were used to view under the cloud cover. This allowed a map to be made of what was happening on the ground. This process is called synthetic aperture **radar**, or SAR. Satellites can see through clouds or smoke, day or night. Tracking a flood accurately can help officials close down important structures such as power stations before flood waters arrive.

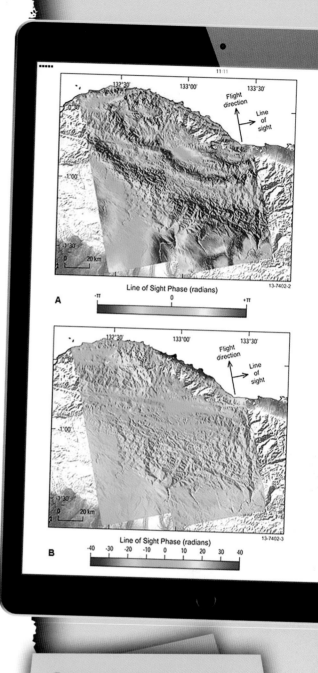

SYNTHETIC APERTURE RADAR (SAR)

is a form of radar that is used to create two-dimensional images or three-dimensional reconstructions of objects such as landscapes.

Responding to Floods

It is **critical** during and after floods for emergency workers to reach people and areas in need. Minutes can save lives. Supplies can prevent sickness and injuries. Having the right people and equipment in the right place at the right time takes planning and organization.

Blockchain for Disasters

Often after a disaster, agencies and organizations from different regions or even countries offer help. But these different groups have no good way to communicate with each other.

Blockchain is a public record created on the Internet. Each time someone creates files of information, or blocks, they become part of the record and can't be changed or deleted. The record continues to grow each time a new block is added. This system has many uses. One use that governments are interested in is disaster relief communication.

Quicker Reaction Time

As each group, organization, company, or service has something to ask for, report, or share, they create a block. Everyone has access to the record, even individuals. This system would allow services to react more quickly and resources to be used where they are needed most. It would also provide a complete record of what was done and where it was done. This information could help researchers make an even better plan for future disasters.

LIDAR for Disasters

Planes flying above a flood have a difficult time recognizing landforms. LIDAR (Light Detection and Ranging) is a special type of radar that can see the ground through trees, plants, and water. LIDAR can help identify roads, vehicles, and places to land a helicopter. Other technologies used for disaster relief are robots and drones. They can help locate survivors and even drop packages with medicine or food. The Serval Project was started in Australia. It uses software that **meshes** together Wi-Fi to allow people to use their cell phones even when there is no mobile phone operator. This could be lifesaving during a disaster when cell phone towers are not working.

LIDAR collects measurements which can then be used to create three-dimensional models and maps of objects and environments. This map was made using LIDAR.

When the Waters Recede

Once floodwaters **recede**, there is more work to be done. Everything damaged, moved, or washed away has to be repaired or replaced. One of the biggest concerns after flooding is mold. Mold is a type of fungus that grows in wet conditions. People can get sick by breathing in spores from mold. Checking for mold after a flood involves taking samples of wood or fabric and testing them in a lab.

Mold Tests

It takes several days for the sample to grow and some types of mold don't grow at all. This makes it very hard to evaluate the risk. However, scientists have developed a new test. It collects air samples on a special type of aluminum foil, then scans them with a very sensitive microscope. The test is very accurate for identifying mold.

FLOOD SAFETY TIPS

BEFORE

STAY INFORMED ON LOCAL NEWS

PREPARE AN EMERGENCY BAG WITH FOOD, DRUGS, DOCUMENTS, FLASHLIGHT, PET ITEMS

KNOW HOW TO EVACUATE AND SAFE ALTERNATIVE ROUTES

LEAVE BEFORE FLOODING STARTS

IN FLOOD PRONE AREAS: KEEP USEFUL ITEMS AT HOME (SANDBAGS, LADDER, ROPE...)

DURING THE FLOOD

DISCONNECT ELECTRICITY AND GAS

DON'T WALK OR DRIVE IN FLOOD WATER

GET TO A HIGHER GROUND

FOLLOW EVACUATION ORDERS

FREE CATTLE AND LEAD ANIMALS TO A SAFER PLACE

AFTER

AVOID CONTACT WITH FLOOD WATER AND SWIMMING

DON'T TOUCH POWER LINES

DON'T GO HOME OR TO DISASTER AREAS UNTIL IT IS DECLARED SAFE

COMMUNICATE TO YOUR FAMILY THAT YOU ARE SAFE

WHEN BACK HOME: CLEAN AND DISINFECT SURFACES AND ITEMS

Mold damage caused by a flood

Future Flood Planning

Flood recovery also means preparing a flood plan for any future events. Schools are encouraged to prepare a flood safety plan for students. It includes

- how to warn staff and students of a flood risk

- a plan to evacuate everyone to a safe location

- protecting the area with items such as inflatable flood barriers

- protecting equipment such as computers and electronics

- having flood insurance

SCIENCE BIO
Tamsin Lyle, Flood Planner

Tamsin Lyle is the principal consultant for Ebbwater, a company that specializes in flood management. She has worked on many flood and risk projects across Canada as both an engineer and a **policy planner**. Tamsin shares what she knows from the many articles she has written on how areas can lower and manage their flood risk. She helps communities realize that the next flood isn't an "if" but a "when." With this knowledge, they can prepare and prevent **catastrophic** damages and loss of life. Her latest presentations are on climate change and rising sea levels.

The work of flood experts such as Tamsin Lyle helps communities protect against major floods.

Knowledge Is Power

Flooding across the world is changing. Climate change is causing more intense storms in some areas and droughts in others. Rising sea levels and melting glaciers are changing land and seascapes and endangering communities that are located near them. The number of areas at risk to flooding is growing. To properly prepare for these disasters, we need up-to-date and accurate information.

Data Leads the Way

The data the National Severe Storms Laboratory (NSSL) studies and collects includes information on floods. Their mission is to understand the causes of flash flooding. They also are working on tools to improve the science behind flash flood forecasts and warnings. This data will help them to improve how well and how quickly they predict floods and warn the affected areas.

Flow Monitoring

ANCHOR is a project that monitors the water flow in rivers across the United States. They have more than 7,000 gauges that use radar and LIDAR to make three-dimensional maps of riverbeds. They can also measure how deep and how fast the water is moving. This data is collected, and even the smallest changes in the shape of the riverbed or the rate of flow is measured. Knowing what is normal for a river system lets researchers quickly know when things are changing. This will help them understand the different factors that cause flooding in different rivers.

The National Severe Storms Laboratory works to improve the accuracy of severe weather warnings and forecasts.

CASE STUDY
Disaster Changes Everything

On January 4, 2010, a massive landslide in a mountainous region of Attabad in northern Pakistan led to flooding that destroyed all or parts of several villages. The slide killed 19 people and **displaced** 1,650. It blocked the Hunza River and created a 13-mile (21 km) lake. The growing lake took over farms and a 15.5-mile (25 km) stretch of the Karakoram Highway, the road link to the rest of the country. After the disaster, researchers found that villages used to supporting themselves had difficulty making a living. The destruction of the highway made it impossible to get crops to market or to easily access health care. Their emotional well-being suffered too, because people worried about making enough money to feed themselves and send their children to school. Rebuilding the highway was completed in 2015 and cost $275 million.

Boats are tied up to trees where a village used to stand. People adapted by using boats to transport people and goods while the highway was being reconstructed.

CHAPTER 4

Facing Future Disaster

Climate change is playing a big role in the strength and number of floods happening around the world. Scientists expect cyclones and hurricanes to increase in strength by up to 10 percent with a 2-degree rise in global temperatures. With a 3- to 4-degree rise in temperature, tropical storms would get more powerful by about 26 percent. A warmer atmosphere holds more water vapor. This means floods will become more powerful and more dangerous.

Worsening Floods

Many areas around the world are already facing their worst floods ever. In 2018, the state of Kerala in India had its worst floods in 100 years. Unusually heavy monsoon rains caused flash floods and landslides. More than 300 people died, hundreds of thousands of homes were washed away, and more than 6,213 miles (10,000 km) of roads were damaged. To prevent dam failure from so much water pressure, 37 of the 42 dams in the state opened their gates to release water. This contributed to even heavier flooding downstream.

People gather to help rescue some of those affected by the floods in Kerala in 2018. Heavy monsoon rains caused the worst flooding in Kerala in nearly a century.

Doctors Without Borders, the International Red Cross, and OXFAM are just some of the organizations that routinely assist during and after floods. Governments around the world also pledge support after disasters.

Disaster Services

Some areas of the world are better able to handle disasters than others because they direct resources to disaster management. Despite being one of the richest countries in the world in private wealth, India's emergency services did not have the resources or infrastructure to help. Roads and rail lines were too damaged to bring relief. Ordinary citizens stepped up to rescue people and provide care.

Relief and Supplies

The United Nations Children's Fund (UNICEF) provides disaster relief around the world. It has been active during floods in Serbia, the Philippines, and Pakistan. UNICEF airlifts relief supplies such as medicine, tents, and food. **Contaminated** water and disease are always big problems after a disaster. UNICEF provides tablets to purify water, and vaccinations for children. Other relief organizations also step in to help after devastating floods.

Save the Trees

Trees and plants naturally prevent floods in several ways. They create a **canopy** to soften rainfall to prevent erosion. Trees take in carbon dioxide, which reduces global warming. Their roots soak up water from a large area. Their roots also help prevent landslides by holding the ground together.

Forests Help Prevent Flooding

When we remove large areas of trees to create farmland or to build roads, runways, or cities, we rob the environment of this protection. Global Forest Watch (GFW) says that millions of acres of forest are lost around the world each year. Protecting and replanting forests is one of the most important factors in slowing climate change.

One study from the universities of Birmingham and Southampton in England showed that replanting forests can have a very positive impact on flooding. By planting trees and shrubs on small streams that feed into a river, water that would normally add to the river levels during a flood is kept back. If 25 to 40 percent of these side stream areas of a river system are reforested, the study finds that floodwater could be lowered by 20 percent. That could prevent a huge amount of damage.

CASE STUDY
Resilient by Design

Resilient by Design consists of nine design teams made up of engineers, architects, community leaders, and local residents. In 2017, they took on the challenge to design solutions to protect communities in the San Francisco Bay area from rising sea levels and severe storms. Some winning projects include creating new city areas on higher ground, and slowly returning coastal areas to natural settings. Another project includes returning areas to marshland where floodwater would naturally go.

Flood resilience projects in the San Francisco Bay area include wetland restoration, and protection of wetlands at the shoreline.

RESTORATION IN PROGRESS

Nowhere to Go

One major challenge in preventing future floods is to reevaluate where and how we build cities. When towns and cities expand into floodplains, we shouldn't be surprised when those areas experience flooding. At least 10 percent of all North Americans live in a high-risk zone for flooding.

The problem is only about half of the people living there know that, and new home buyers do not have a reliable way of finding out. Most flood zone maps are about 25 years old. River routes change over time. New locations for mines, hydroelectric dams, farming, and reservoirs are created. This changes where and how fast a river flows. New maps would identify changing flood zones. City officials could then restrict building in these areas.

Flood-Resistant Technology

We should think not only about where we are building our towns and cities, but how. The downtown areas of most cities are a sea of pavement and concrete. Parking garages, apartment buildings, highways, and office buildings grow into each other, leaving almost no soil or grass. Covering over all natural surfaces will give water no place to soak into the ground.

FLOODPLAINS *are a part of rivers and hold water underground. Building on them disconnects rivers from their natural courses and reduces the area's ability to hold water during storms.*

Levees and floodwalls keep water out, but also cause water to rise higher and flow faster than normal.

SCIENCE BIO
Professor Jim Hall

Jim Hall is Professor of Climate and Environmental Risks at Oxford University in England. He has an interest in flood risk, or the identification of actions and measures that could be taken to lessen or prevent floods. He looks at the structures and systems cities have in place to see if they could withstand heavy flooding. Hall has written many papers on climate change and the risk of climate-related flooding. He also speaks at seminars and conferences about how cities can protect themselves from floods.

Seawalls can be used to protect cities and towns that are built near the sea from flooding.

Copenhagen, Denmark, has worked to include areas in the city that can work either dry or flooded. Enghaveparken is a public park surrounded by a large dike. When the park is dry, people can enjoy public areas. With heavy rainfall or flooding, the park can hold 847,552 cubic feet (24,000 cubic m) of water. This is about the same as the amount of water in 10 Olympic-size swimming pools.

Get Flood Ready

Even though there are many new technologies being developed, we are still very unprepared for floods. Flooding is now the costliest cause of damage to homes and businesses in North America. Over the past 10 years, flooding and heavy rains have risen 50 percent around the world, according to a study by the European Academies' Science Advisory Council (EASAC).

International Assistance

A Danish research paper outlined a plan to help poorer countries around the world face natural disasters. For the 34 countries that experience flooding very often, the paper's authors suggest raising all houses off the ground by 3 feet (1 m). They also suggest building floodwalls around communities at risk. They figure that if even just some floodwalls were built, it would cost $75 billion. But not having to repair damage over and over again would save $4.5 trillion. It would also save about 20,000 lives.

The paper also suggests that international **donors** should pay for these measures because preventing flood disasters helps everyone. Fewer relief groups would need to travel to help, and less money would need to be sent to charities to help people afterward.

Flooding around the world has increased by

50%

in the last

10 YEARS

Raising houses off the ground can protect against flood damage.

Weather radar station in the United States

Weather station in Thailand

Early Warnings

Other studies show that early warning systems in all areas of the world would save money and lives. Networks of sensors along waterways can give accurate and quick data when the flow or height of a river begins to change. Early warnings give people and cities time to protect their property, pets, belongings, and family members. The most damage is done when people do not have time to prepare. Advanced weather radar stations are also important. With better technology, storms that might bring heavy rainfall or a high ocean storm surge can be predicted. Better communication systems, especially in less-developed countries, will allow warnings and information to be shared quickly.

CHAPTER 5

Building Resilience

Everyone's Problem

Floods are a worldwide problem. The best way to prevent global disasters is for countries to share their knowledge and technologies. Good communication means we can learn from the past, learn what is working or not working in different areas, and develop and use new technologies. With a changing climate and environment bringing more flooding, we have to learn to adapt. Flood control is not just a problem for governments or communities. It is an individual problem, too. We can all do our part to lessen the impact of flooding. On our own property we can make sure we do not contribute to climate change by limiting our use of fossil fuels—including how we use power in our homes. We can support companies that show their commitment to a greener Earth. We can volunteer to clean up parks and waterways, or to plant trees. We can also add our voices to those petitioning governments and companies to make changes that reduce our risk of flooding and lessen the impact of natural disasters.

The aftermath of a flash flood in a Spanish village

In the last

20 YEARS,

flooding has been the most common natural disaster, accounting for

43%

of all recorded natural disaster events.

Ask Yourself This

Based on the information in this book, what are some of the things humans have learned from devastating floods and their aftereffects?

1. Why should we study flood events that happen in other parts of the world? What can they teach us?

2. Many regions have set up sensors along waterways to monitor water levels. They are placed along public rivers and canals. The Flood Network in England uses data from sensors set on private property. What are the advantages of using a system of data collection from private residents? What are the disadvantages?

3. Do you know if you live in a flood zone? How can you find out? What sort of preparations should you make as a personal flood plan?

Bibliography

Introduction

Mogil, H. Michael. *Extreme Weather*. New York: Simon & Schuster Books for Young Readers, 2011.

Nunez, Christina. "Floods, explained." *National Geographic*, April 4, 2019. https://on.natgeo.com/2Bio6x4

World Meteorological Organization. https://public.wmo.int/en

Chapter 1

Chris Zevenbergen PhD. www.un-ihe.org/chris-zevenbergen

Erdman, Jon. "The World's Deepest Snows." *The Weather Channel*, February 11, 2015. https://wxch.nl/2Iylh1o

"Five things to know about flooding and climate change." Carbon Brief, November 27, 2012. https://bit.ly/2Jes8wb

Global Flood Awareness System. www.globalfloods.eu

"The Science of Floods." *PBS Newshour Extra*, September 1, 1997. https://to.pbs.org/2IAB4N4

Chapter 2

Calgary Herald. *The Flood of 2013: A Summer of Angry Rivers in Southern Alberta*. Vancouver: Greystone Books, 2013.

Courtney, Chris. "Central China flood, 1931." Disaster History. www.disasterhistory.org/central-china-flood-1931

"Final Report on 1998 Floods in the People's Republic of China." Reliefweb, September 29, 1998. https://bit.ly/2L3atKi

Global Water Futures. https://gwf.usask.ca

Schwartz, John, and Mark Schleifstein. "Fortified But Still in Peril, New Orleans Braces for Its Future." *The New York Times*, February 24, 2018. https://nyti.ms/2otqzkr

Chapter 3

Fisheries and Oceans Canada. https://bit.ly/2Y2cA4F

Flood Network. https://flood.network

NASA Global Flood Monitoring System. https://go.nasa.gov/2N5ycw6

National Severe Storms Laboratory (NSSL). www.nssl.noaa.gov

Paynter, Ben. "This tech tells cities when floods are coming—and what they will destroy." Fast Company, April 8, 2019. https://bit.ly/31NkqkX

Rohr, Jeanette. "Blockchain For Disaster Relief: Creating Trust Where It Matters Most." *Digitalist Magazine*, November 23, 2017. https://bit.ly/2Y2iFy8

Serval Project. www.servalproject.org

Tamsin Lyle, Principal. https://bit.ly/2kPwHon

Watson, Barbara, Stephen Kuhl, Dave Nicosia, Ray O'Keefe, and Brian Montgomery. "When the Weather Turns Severe: A Guide to Developing a Severe Weather Emergency Plan for Schools." NOAA/ National Weather Service, May 2018. https://bit.ly/2IxQ7qK

Chapter 4

"Disaster and Emergency Relief." UNICEF. https://bit.ly/2xbq7Lk

"Enghavenparken Now". https://bit.ly/2lXUgLH

"Global Forest Resources Assessment." Food and Agriculture Organization of the United Nations. www.fao.org/forest-resources-assessment/en

Global Forest Watch. www.globalforestwatch.org

"Jim Hall–Robust decisions under uncertainty: examples of info-gap analysis in mitigation policy and flood risk management." The London School of Economics and Political Science, June 3, 2010. https://bit.ly/2WXhXRj

Lomborg, Bjørn. "An Ounce of Prevention." Slate. May 4, 2012. https://bit.ly/2J3SL6y

"New UNESCO project aims to improve early warnings for floods in Pakistan." UN News. July 13, 2011. https://bit.ly/2WTkGLC

Resilient by Design Bay Area Challenge. www.resilientbayarea.org

Learning More

Books

Abdo, Kenny. *How to Survive a Flood.* ABDO Zoom, 2018.

Baker, John R. *The World's Worst Floods.* Capstone Press, 2016.

Eagan, Rachel. *Flood and Monsoon Alert.* Crabtree Publishing, 2011.

Thomas, Keltie. *Rising Seas: Flooding, Climate Change and Our New World.* Firefly Books, 2018.

Websites

Learn about flooding with National Geographic Kids: **https://bit.ly/2L9oBSd**

Flood safety tips with Weather WizKids: **www. weatherwizkids.com/ weather-safety-flood.htm**

Let NASA explain how predicting floods is getting better with their new satellite: **https://go.nasa. gov/2eSL18L**

Enter your address on the flood map to see if you are in a flood zone: **https://bit.ly/2tN3xrU**

Glossary

absorb To soak up

acoustic Having to do with sound or hearing

artificial intelligence Computers that are able to think like humans

canopy The upper layer of leaves and branches on a group of trees

catastrophic Involving sudden great damage or suffering

contaminated Not pure

critical Of the greatest importance

cyclones Strong tropical storms, also called hurricanes

debris Loose natural material and waste

deforestation Cutting down trees and clearing the land

delta A low, triangular area where a river meets the sea

dikes Long walls built to prevent flooding

displaced Forced to leave an area

donors People who give money to a charity

droughts Long periods of no rain

evacuate To remove from danger to a safer place

forecasting Calculating what may happen in the future

fossil fuels Fuels made from petroleum or oil, gas, and coal that when burned create greenhouse gases that warm Earth

infrastructure Things such as transportation, buildings, communications, and power supplies that a society needs to function

levees Structures built to prevent the overflow of a river

meltwater Water from melting ice and snow

mesh To fit or work together

microscopic life Tiny organisms that can only be seen with a microscope

monitored Observed and reported on

policy planner A person in charge of creating a course of action

predict To make a rough guess about what might happen in the future

radar A device that sends out radio waves for finding the position and speed of a moving object

recede To move back

Red Cross/Red Crescent A collection of groups that help people during times of war and natural disasters

sediment Small pieces of dirt and rock in water

severe Extreme and very serious

storm surges Rises in the sea level from the winds of coming storms

tributaries Small streams that flow into a river

United Nations An organization made up of 193 countries that works to promote peace and human rights around the world

urban Having to do with a town or city

wetlands Areas that have standing water, such as swamps or marshes

Index

About the Author

Natalie Hyde remembers a flood in her hometown when she was a child. She saw shoes from the local department store floating down the river. She hopes the new technology mentioned in this book prevents it from ever happening again.